A SPECTACULAR SEEK AND FIND CHALLENGE FOR ALL AGES!

BiGFOOT™
Goes On Vacation

D. L. MILLER

HAPPY FOX
BOOKS™

For Mom and Dad, and the Miller brothers who grew up in our little house nestled in the mountains of Western Maryland, where we spent many a day exploring the beauty and mysteries of the woods and creek bottoms just outside our front door.

— D. L. Mill

A Big Thank You
to all the BigFoot hunters around the world who not only believe that our big furry friend really does exist, but more importantly that he continues to inspire us to go outside and explore this great big world.

A Special Thank You
to the wonderful folks at Fox Chapel Publishing for bringing the BigFoot Seek and Find series to life, especially…

Publisher: Alan Giagnocavo
Vice President – Content: Christopher Reggio
Senior Editor: Laura Taylor
Managing Editor: Melissa Younger
Contributing Editor: Jeremy Hauck
Graphic Design: Kate Lanphier

© 2017, 2018 by D. L. Miller and Happy Fox Books, an imprint of Fox Chapel Publishing Company, Inc., 903 Square Street, Mount Joy, PA 17552.

BigFoot Goes on Vacation is an original work, first published in 2018 by Fox Chapel Publishing Company, Inc.

ISBN 978-1-64124-000-0

The Cataloging-in-Publication Data is on file with the Library of Congress.

To learn more about the other great books from Fox Chapel Publishing, or to find a retailer near you, call toll-free 800-457-9112 or visit us at *www.FoxChapelPublishing.com*.

We are always looking for talented authors. To submit an idea, please send a brief inquiry to acquisitions@foxchapelpublishing.com.

Printed in China
First printing

Shutterstock photos: Anatol Pietryczuk (38 top); Andrey Krupenko (31 top); Andrzej Kubik (14 top); Aneta Waberska (26 bottom lower inset); Australonico (19 middle left); Autumn Sky Photography (34 upper middle); AVA Bitter (38 middle); Benny Marty (15 bottom); Bill45 (18 middle); blvdone (22 middle right); Brent Hofacker (11 upper center, 11 lower center); Chris Parypa Photography (26 middle); Christopher MacDonald (35 bottom); Damsea (19 top); Dariush M (10 top right); Darryl Brooks (10 middle); Dudarev Mikhail (35 upper middle); Eduard Kyslynskyy (14 mid center); Eirik Gumeny (31 upper middle right); Elena Yakusheva (30 bottom right); Elivagar (7 top); ER_09 (7 bottom); Gary L. Brewer (11 top); GERARD BOTTINO (6 bottom); gvictoria (31 mid center); Happy Stock Photo (43 bottom); hutch photography (30 top); Innalex (30 middle right); Jag_cz (39 upper top right); Joop Hoek (34 top); karamysh (42 top); Kate Sfeir (35 top); kavram (22 top); Kelly vanDellen (34 bottom); Kenneth Sponsler (11 bottom); Kidd Silencer (43 middle); Kris Wiktor (23 middle left); Krishna Utkarsh Pandit (15 top); lauraslens (26 top); Leah-Anne Thompson (6 top); Liubov Usmanova (23 middle right); LuminatePhotos by judith (15 middle left); Macier 3 Photography (27 bottom); Manamana (39 bottom); Marek Gucwa (14 bottom); Marina Parshina (31 bottom); Mark Agnor (19 bottom); Mark Van Scyoc (22 middle left); Maryna Kulchytska (27 top inset); Michelle Holihan (23 top); mrcmos (35 lower middle); Nagel Photography (23 bottom); nfmlk (27 top); OH_HO (30 bottom left); Oleg Chegodaev (6 bottom inset); Olga Visavi (19 middle right); Patino (10 top left); Pawel Kazmierczak (42 middle left); Perry Correll (26 bottom upper inset); Petr Bonek (38 bottom); PLRANG ART (6 top inset); Popsidoodle (35 bottom inset); Poznyakov (42 middle right); Ramunas Bruzas (27 middle right); Rudy Riva (5 top right); RugliG (27 middle left); Sean Locke Photography (43 top right); smereka (31 middle left); sondzr (34 lower middle); Stig Alenas (39 lower top right); StockStudio (7 middle); structuresxx (11 mid center); Tai-mOn (18 bottom); Tonis Valing (26 bottom); topseller (31 lower middle right); tornadoflight (42 bottom); travelview (43 top left); Vector Tradition SM (39 top left); Vera Petruk (5 bottom); Villiers Steyn (14 upper center); Vinicius Bacarin (30 middle left); Volodymyr Burdiak (14 lower center, 15 middle right); Yasonya (31 top inset); Zacchio (30 top inset)

BiGFOOT CONTENTS

The new things we see and do on vacation give us so much to talk about when we get back. So get your suitcase ready, because it's time to see the great outdoors—BigFoot style!

HOW TO USE THIS BOOK

Read a bit about different vacation spots. You may learn something surprising!

Turn the page and search for BigFoot. The keys along the sides tell you what else to look for. Good luck!

WHO IS BIGFOOT?

Stories about the infamous BigFoot have been handed down from generation to generation in many countries around the world. Although his history is a bit **unknown**, many theories have been explored over the years to explain why people continue to see this mysterious creature no matter where they live. Some believe he's a **giant bear** that has been seen walking around on two legs, while others believe he may be a **giant gorilla** roaming the forests.

HAVE YOU SEEN A REAL BiGFOOT?

Although descriptions of the giant, fury creature differ from region to region, they all share several common details: a large, fury human-like creature standing **7 feet (2.3 m) to 9 feet (3 m) tall**. Reports suggest that BigFoot is brown, although many have also reported seeing black, gray, white, and greenish-blue BigFoots. Some descriptions also include details such as **large eyes** with a very pronounced brow, and a large forehead. The top of his head is often described as rounded with a narrow top, similar to the shape of a large gorilla. If you see someone walking around that looks like this, you're probably looking at BigFoot!

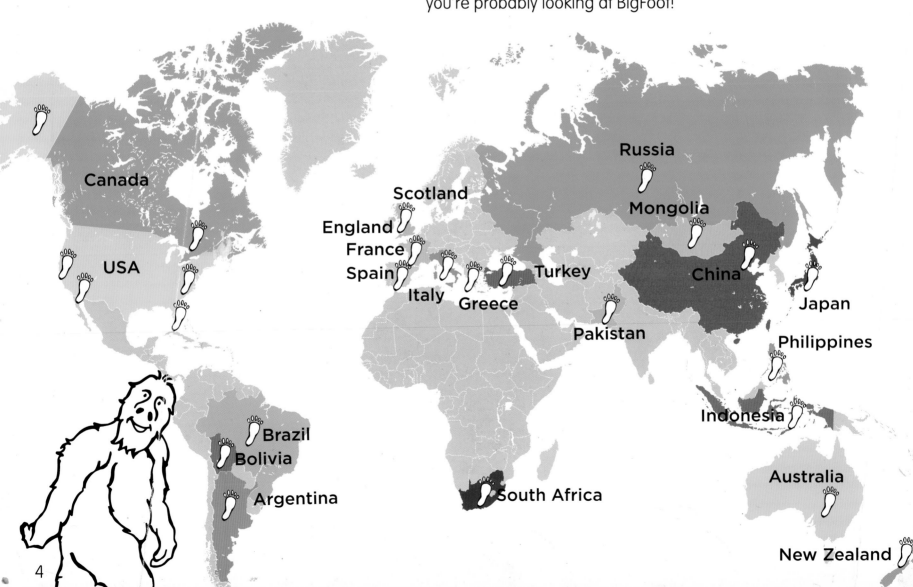

Canada

USA

Scotland

England

France

Spain

Italy

Greece

Turkey

Russia

Mongolia

China

Japan

Philippines

Pakistan

Indonesia

Brazil

Bolivia

Argentina

South Africa

Australia

New Zealand

Frame 352 of the Patterson-Gimlin film, taken in the fall of 1967 in Northern California's **Six Rivers National Forest** by Roger Patterson and Bob Gimlin. While some people believe the **BigFoot** shown here was only a person in a costume, others believe it's the real deal.

BIG FOOT XING

DUE TO SIGHTINGS IN THE AREA OF A CREATURE RESEMBLING "BIG FOOT" THIS SIGN HAS BEEN POSTED FOR YOUR SAFETY

WHERE DiD THE NAME BiGFOOT COME FROM?

In the 1800s, the name *BigFoot* was first used in America to describe huge **grizzly bears** that were spotted in parts of the United States. Some believe that **David Thompson**, a man crossing the Rocky Mountains in the winter of 1811, discovered the first real set of BigFoot footprints in the snow. The tracks were too big for even the largest known bear. The name was again used when people started spotting massive, **human-like** footprints on the forest floor that kind of resembled a large bear's. These footprints were about 24 inches (61 cm) long and 8 inches (20 cm) wide, more than **double** the size of an average adult shoe. Many people believe that these big footprints are enough proof that our BigFoot really does exist!

It's been reported by some that BigFoot can run up to 30 miles per hour (48 kph)—the average human runs half that speed!

BiGFOOT GOES BY MANY NAMES

BigFoot is known by many different names around the world, including the most common: **Sasquatch**. So don't forget to tell people you're going **"Squatching"** next time you decide to search for our giant, furry friend. What do other parts of the world call BigFoot?

Barmanou (Pakistan)

Basajuan (Spain)

Big Greyman (Scotland)

Gin-Sung (China)

Hibagon (Japan)

Kapre (Philippines)

Kushtaka (Alaska, USA)

Mapinguari (Brazil and Bolivia)

Menk (Russia)

Moehau (New Zealand)

Mogollon Monster (Arizona, USA)

Orange Pendek (Indonesia)

Skunk Ape (Florida, USA)

Ucu (Argentina)

Waterbobbejaan (South Africa)

Wendigo (Canada)

Woodwosa (England)

Yeren (Mongolia)

Yeti (Russia)

Yowie (Australia)

IX

9 THE HERMIT
YETI

Cruise

READY TO CRUISE

When a cruise ship *docks*, or parks alongside land, the ship's crew has to make sure it doesn't drift back out to sea. Using ropes called *mooring lines* ("mooring" means to make a boat sit still), they tie the ship to the *wharf*, or the place where boats line up so passengers can exit and be on land. The mooring lines are wrapped around posts called *bollards*. Tied tightly, the ropes keep the ship, no matter how big, snug in place. When passengers leave the ship, they walk down *gangplanks*, little footbridges that can be packed up and carried on the ship when it's time to go again.

HARMONY OF THE SEAS

The **biggest** cruise ship in the world, called *Harmony of the Seas*, can carry **5,479 passengers** and has 23 swimming pools, 24 restaurants, and replicas of both New York's Central Park and the Atlantic City Boardwalk. It's **1,188 feet** (362 m) long and has 2,747 cabins ("cabins" are like hotel rooms on a ship). To serve the passengers' needs—by cooking meals, cleaning cabins, steering the ship, and so on—a **staff of 2,300 people** goes along, too. But before the *Harmony* leaves the wharf, it has to be loaded with all the food and supplies it will need during its voyage. There's no running to the market for anything when you're in the middle of the ocean on a cruise ship!

There's no reason to ever be bored on a cruise ship. Bumper cars, movies, live theater—the modern cruise ship could practically be called **"Entertainmentville"**! For example, the *Harmony* has a waterpark with a 100-foot waterslide—fun!

EARLY CRUISES

Before airplanes became a common way to travel in the late 1950s, cruising on a ship wasn't just for vacation; it was the **only** way to cross the ocean! Some ships, of course, were nicer than others.

In 1949, a British ship called the *Caronia* became the **first luxury ship** designed to take people on leisurely cruises without having any real point-to-point purpose. It was **715 feet** (218 m) long and carried **932 passengers**. But it was only in the 1970s that cruise vacations really began to take off. Ships got bigger and bigger, more and more on-board activities were added, and ships headed exclusively to places like the Mediterranean, the Alaskan coast, and the Caribbean.

A knot is one nautical mile per hour (1.25 mph per knot). The nautical mile is 6,076 feet (1,852 m). That means cruise ships "cruise" at about 25 miles (40 km) per hour.

WHERE ARE YOU ON A SHIP?

The **sides** of a ship have names that may seem unusual at first, but if you spend much time at sea and get used to saying them, they'll start to sound natural!

Front = Bow

Right side = Starboard

Left side = Port

Back = Stern

Bow   Starboard   Stern

Port

The different levels of a ship are called *decks*—like the floors of a building. The place where the captain sits is called the *bridge*. It has all the tools needed to steer the ship across the ocean. **GPS** (global positioning system) shows the captain where storms are and where the ship is sailing at any given moment. **Sonar** shows what's underwater and how deep the water is. Radar systems track other ships in the area, even at night, and radio and cell phones allow the captain to stay in touch with other ships and with people on land.

BiGFOOT
Takes a Cruise

1 BigFoot

1 Legendary Footprint

5 Passengers with Pink Luggage

3 Bashful Captains

5 Polly Parrots

6 Coconut Trees

6 Dancing Hula Girls

10 Orange Sailboats

9 Passengers with Green Hat & Pack

Carnival

ONCE UPON A CARNIVAL . . .

In places like New Orleans, Louisiana; Rio de Janeiro, Brazil; and Venice, Italy, *carnival* means a festive time of partying before the traditional Roman Catholic fasting season of **Lent**. People wear masks and play lots of music and perform in colorful parades. It is from this type of carnival that clowns and stilts-wearing masked entertainers come from.

But most American carnivals are more properly called **"fairs."** The American fair tradition began in 1811, when well-traveled businessman **Elkanah Watson** organized a gathering of farmers in **Pittsfield, Massachusetts**, to celebrate country living. Today, the biggest state fair in the United States is held in **Dallas, Texas**, which draws more than **2.5 million** people every October. Events include pig races, milking demonstrations, and a nighttime parade. And, of course, lots of delicious food!

In 2006, Saimaiti Yiming (China) walked 10 steps on his own on the tallest stilts ever mastered: 53 ft 10 in (16.41 m).

CLASSIC RIDES

Bumper cars: Powered by electricity circulated through a wire mesh roof and down to the cars through flexible poles, sparks can sometimes fly, making it smell like ozone as you look for more people to ram into.

Tilt-a-whirl: Cram a few people in a little pod that spins crazily in tight circles, famous for causing motion sickness—hopefully BigFoot doesn't get sick easily!

Ferris wheel: Best part is getting the birds-eye view at the top and trying to spot your friends on the ground.

TASTY TREATS

At carnivals, the food is very bad for you but tastes very good!
Some amazing carnival foods you're probably a fan of:

Deep-fried butter balls, made from scoops of butter that are battered and deep-fried

Funnel cakes, snowed over with powdered sugar

Chocolate-covered bacon on a stick, made from fried bacon dipped in chocolate and skewered

Cotton candy, spun flavored sugar

Ice cream cheeseburger, a cheeseburger topped with a scoop of ice cream that has been coated in corn flakes and deep-fried

Corndogs, made from skewered hotdogs dipped in cornmeal batter then deep-fried

Fried Oreos, an Oreo that is dipped in batter and deep-fried.

YUM!

Most Ferris wheels at carnivals today are much smaller than the original, with a typical diameter of 50 feet (15 m).

BIRTH OF THE MIDWAY

The part of a fair where most of the rides, games, and food stands are clustered is typically called the **"midway,"** a name that came from the **Chicago World's Fair,** which opened on **May 1, 1893.** One of the areas at the fair was called the Midway Pleasance, which people shortened to just "the Midway." The Midway was a **mile long** and featured exhibits on cultures from around the world. But the exhibits took second place to something much more fun: a wheel ride **250 feet** (76 m) across that could carry more than 1,000 people at a time, giving those at the top the best view of Chicago they'd ever seen. The wheel, designed for the fair by **George W. G. Ferris,** immediately became the symbol of the American carnival.

11

BiGFOOT

Visits the Carnival

1 BigFoot

1 Legendary Footprint

6 Giggling Clowns

7 Kids with Cotton Candy

5 Balloon Sellers

8 Girls with Heart Balloons

8 Feeding Pigeons

3 Wandering Coyotes

5 Steady Stilt Walkers

African Plains

When people visit the African plains, it's often called going **"on safari."** The word *safari* derives from the Arabic word for **taking a journey**, *safar*. The African plains is a **savannah** environment, which means it is mostly flat, mostly grassy, and warm for most of the year. Aside from two rainy seasons, the African plains are **dry**. About half of Africa is covered in **grassy plains**. When going on safari, you'll see beautiful scenery and all kinds of amazing animals in their natural habitat.

DID YOU KNOW?

A **lion's** roar can be heard up to 5 miles (8 km) away.

Elephants flap their ears to help cool themselves.

The longest **rhinoceros** tusk discovered was 59 inches (150 cm) long.

Leopards are nocturnal—they hunt and eat at night.

A **giraffe** has a black tongue so it doesn't get sunburned when using it to grasp food in tall trees.

Africa's **biggest mammals** are so important that enormous land areas have been set aside just for them. For example, the **Great Limpopo Transfrontier Park** spanning parts of Mozambique, Zimbabwe, and South Africa is **14,500** square miles (37,000 km²), making it an animal country that's about twice the size of New Jersey!

WONDROUS ECOSYSTEM

Over thousands of years, the animals of the African **grassland plains** have become used to living with each other, and they each play a part in keeping their natural home clean and safe. If the trees and shrubs start to take over an area, the elephants go to work and **bulldoze**. If the herd animals like zebras, Cape buffalo, or antelopes become too numerous and start to eat too much of the grass that protects the earth, lions, leopards, and cheetahs pounce.

Swahili ("of the coast") people live in central East Africa, close enough to the Arabian peninsula for frequent trading. So their language borrows a lot of words from Arabic: *simba* (lion), for example.

TERRIFIC TREES

Acacia trees (top photo) are shaped like umbrellas to collect sun and provide shade. They can tolerate long, dry seasons and hot days. Acacia trees produce a substance called **gum Arabic**, which is used to make things like paint, candy, makeup, and medicine! **Giraffes** use their long tongues to nibble at the leaves at the top of these trees. When the acacia flowers bloom, the giraffes have a feast. In the lower branches, **cheetahs** love to take catnaps, keeping one eye on the plains for a possible meal.

Thick-trunked **baobab** trees (bottom photo) stand out in the landscape like watchtowers—and, since birds love to perch on them, they are often full of eyes! Their trunks hold a large amount of water, so some safari animals like **elephants** will chew the bark if there's no watering hole nearby. Baobab trunks are so large—one is on record with a **154-foot** (47-m) circumference—they have been hollowed out and used as a post office and a jail!

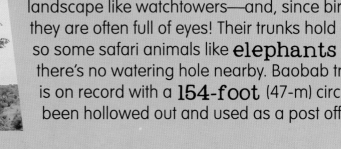

BiGFOOT

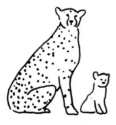

1 BigFoot

1 Legendary Footprint

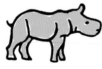

3 Baby Rhinos

3 Proud Cheetahs with Baby

3 Safari Adventure Groups

4 Whacky Jackals

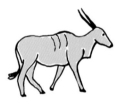

8 Anxious Antelopes

5 Alert Buzzards

10 Gliding Buzzards

Deep Sea Diving

THE BLUE EARTH

Oceans cover **71 percent** of the Earth's surface. Imagine if the entire world were a house with 10 bedrooms, and all the animals lived in those 10 rooms. **Ocean animals**—humpback whales, jellyfish, sharks, corals, and even tiny plankton—would occupy 7 of those rooms, and all the other animals, including you and all your friends (and maybe BigFoot!) would fit into the other 3 rooms.

Male seahorses, not the females, give birth to baby seahorses.

DIVING DEEP

When you go **deep sea diving**, you will be moving downward in deep water—you'll need to wear a special waterproof diving suit and breathing gear. Divers can wear a **helmet** with a breathing tube connected to an air supply on a boat at the water's surface. Or in **scuba diving**, the diver wears a **mask** connected by a hose to a tank of air worn like a backpack—no need to be connected to anything on the surface. Scuba divers who are just diving for fun don't go deeper than around **130 feet** (40 m). Explorers and scientists go deep underwater by riding in a specially made ship like a **submarine**, which has air to breathe for a set amount of time, navigation systems, food, and sometimes even small beds!

Divers use SCUBA gear to breath underwater. SCUBA is an acronym for "self-contained underwater breathing apparatus."

THE LIVING OCEAN

There are different categories of ocean animals. *Benthic* animals live their whole lives on the bottom of the ocean, in what marine biologists call the **"benthic realm."** Some of these creatures crawl or swim across the ocean floor while others, like the staghorn coral of the Caribbean, live attached to it. Sea animals that swim freely throughout the ocean are called *nektonic* animals, or nektons. With fins and tails and tentacles, these creatures move their bodies through the water to get from place to place, just as we use our arms and legs to swim.

Orcas travel in groups called pods. The pods are led by females, and they are highly talkative, even to the point of having different languages among pods.

Scientists recently discovered a "town" off the eastern coast of Australia where 15 octopuses talk to each other and hang out together. The scientists named the settlement "Octlantis."

SUBMARINES

Using submarines is the only way **scientists** can see what lies on the bottom of the deepest parts of the ocean. Submarines are also used by the **military** to protect its ships and by researchers looking for artifacts in sunken ships. So how do submarines stay underwater? A submarine has a compartment called a **ballast** tank that fills with water so the sub becomes heavier and can sink. When the crew is ready to rise to the surface, they drain the ballast, which makes the submarine light enough to rise.

BiGFOOT
Goes Deep Sea Diving

1 Deep Sea BigFoot

1 Legendary Footprint

3 Playful Orcas

4 Sassy Sea Turtles

13 Galloping Seahorses

10 Red Tank Scuba Divers

5 Yellow Submarines

8 Awesome Octopuses

5 Dapper Dolphins

12 Drifting Jellyfish

Yellowstone

THE FIRST NATIONAL PARK

Established in **1872**, Yellowstone was the first national park in the United States—and in the world, too. Taking up **3,472 square miles** (8,991 km²) of Idaho, Montana, and Wyoming (mostly Wyoming), Yellowstone is larger than Rhode Island and Delaware combined. The park has visitor centers, campgrounds, and picnic areas. All kinds of mammals, birds, fish, reptiles, and amphibians live in Yellowstone. You can see many of these animals and the beautiful landscape from **1,000 miles** (1,600 km) of trails in the park—bring your hiking boots, water, and camera!

As big as it is, Yellowstone is not even the biggest national park in the United States—it's actually the **8th biggest**. Six of the parks bigger than Yellowstone are in Alaska; the remaining one is California's Death Valley National Park.

SLEEPING VOLCANO

Yellowstone National Park sits on top of a **volcano!** The land formation you can see on the surface is called a ***caldera***, a shallow circular bowl **30 miles** (48 km) wide. This caldera was made when the volcano erupted around 640,000 years ago. The last time this volcano erupted was **174,000** years ago. The presence of the park's many **geysers** shows there's plenty of heat still below ground, and the thousands of earthquakes that occur in the park each year prove that there is still activity below this volcano. But scientists believe the volcano won't erupt again for thousands of years—good news!

OLD FAITHFUL

A **geyser** is a spring that shoots up hot water and steam every now and then. The most famous geyser ever might just be **Yellowstone's Old Faithful**. It erupts about every 90 minutes, shooting hot water up about **170 feet** (52 m) in the air. Don't touch it! The water that Old Faithful sprays is **204°F** (96°C)!

NATURE'S ART STUDIO

Each geyser has its own palette of colors to show you what ingredients are in its watery mineral soup. A **mineral** is a substance that is not a plant or an animal. Where the water looks green, there is **yellow sulfur** mixing with blue water. Red-colored water shows that **iron** is in it. White step-like formations have **limestone**.

Every year, more people visit Yellowstone. In 2016, more than 4.2 million visitors came to the park.

WHERE THE BISON ROAM

Is it *buffalo* or *bison*? Well, they're the same thing! **Buffalo** is simply a more casual way to refer to the animal known to scientists as *Bison bison*. The buffalo is the biggest land mammal on the North American continent, weighing up to **2,000 pounds** (907 kg). There are two herds of buffalo in Yellowstone: the **northern herd** and the **central herd**. Descended from the buffalo grazing in the Yellowstone area since prehistoric times when dinosaurs roamed the land, the Yellowstone herds are revered by Native American tribes. Nearly **5,000** wild buffalos are in Yellowstone at any given time.

With about 11 wolf packs, just over a hundred wild wolves are roaming the park. Elk is their main source of food. Lucky for them, there are close to 5,000 elk in Yellowstone!

23

BiGFOOT

Visits Yellowstone

1 BigFoot

1 Legendary Footprint

11 Passing Elks

5 Helpful Park Rangers

 **14** Roaming Buffalos

 6 Howling Wolves

 **8** Giant Grizzly Bears

 **7** Resting Rams

 **6** Hikers with Green Jackets

BEAUTIFUL BEACHES

Whether you call them beaches or shores, there are more than **200 million** miles of them in the world, and each one has its own character. Some beaches are packed with people but others are deserted except for hermit crabs and seagulls. But all beaches share some things in common: the soothing sound of **waves**, bright sunlight reflecting off the water, and the tangy smell of the **salt** air.

Beaches around the world have different names: *strand* (German, Swedish, Dutch); *playa* (Spanish); *plage* (French); *pwani* (Swahili).

LET'S GO TO THE BEACH!

Around **8 million** people a year go to the beach at **Ocean City**, Maryland—home of boardwalk fries topped with Old Bay seasoning and malt vinegar. Even more people—around **17 million**—head to **Myrtle Beach**, South Carolina, each year. Then there are all of the popular beaches in Florida, New Jersey, California, and Hawaii, and the rest of the world. Heading to the beach may be the most popular kind of vacation!

SHORELINE TREASURES

Lightning whelks: a beautiful spiraled seashell narrowing to an open point, formerly home to a sea snail

Sand dollars: related to a sea urchin, lives 6 to 10 years in the wild

Beach glass or mermaid's tears: bits of glass polished smooth by the waves

26

WHAT IS SAND?

What we see as sand is millions of tiny **rock grains** less than 2 millimeters across—small enough to be blown by wind. Sand grains started out as bigger pebbles and stones that became smaller over time—thousands of years—as waves and wind ground them down. Typical **tan sand** is mostly made up of **quartz**—hard clusters of 6-sided crystals made up of oxygen and silicon atoms. **White sand,** however, comes mostly from the shells of coral and other sea creatures. **Black sand** comes from **basalt**—rock that came out of a volcano.

TIDES COME AND GO

When the ocean **water level** rises or falls, these times are called **high tide** or **low tide**. The tides are caused by the sun and moon's **gravitational pull** on the water and also by the **Earth's rotation**. At high tide, the ocean water will be farther up on the beach—you may need to move your chair and umbrella in a hurry!

SEAGULLS

Have you ever swallowed saltwater when you're in the ocean? **Yuck!** Seagulls have a special ability that we don't have: they can **drink saltwater** and survive just fine on it. If you see a seagull up close, look at its bill: usually there will be clear liquid hanging from the tip. When seagulls drink saltwater, the salt is absorbed in their **bloodstream,** passes through special **glands** above their eyes, and moves out of the body through the **nostrils** in the bill. **Amazing!**

Low Tide

High Tide

While still in the egg, a pelican chick can let their parent know if it's too cold or too hot!

BiGFOOT

Spotted at the Beach

1 BigFoot

1 Legendary Footprint

4 Sassy Sea Turtles

16 Sneaky Seagulls

8 Sand Castles

10 Yellow Jet Skis

8 Friendly Pelicans

8 Umbrella Swimmers

12 Blue-Trunk Swimmers

Farm

RURAL GETAWAY

Why would you vacation on a farm? There are so many reasons! Leave the noisy city behind and enjoy the **fresh air,** cute animals, delicious food, and a hundred other cool things on a farm—here are just a few great **activities** to try:

Milk a cow

Feed a pig

Plant seeds

Hug a lamb

Play in the creek

Ride on a tractor

Make a scarecrow

Go fishing in a pond

Pick your own berries

Collect eggs

Make ice cream

Spin wool

Ride a horse

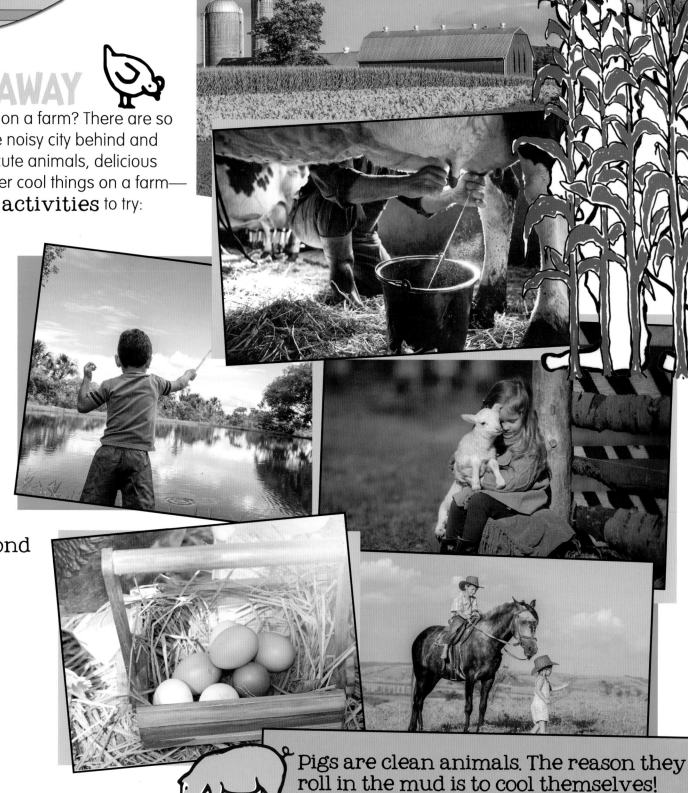

Pigs are clean animals. The reason they roll in the mud is to cool themselves!

CORN

Corn comes from a wild **grass plant** native to Central and South America called *Zea mays*, and it is believed that corn was first grown more than **9,000 years** ago. Corn can be eaten many ways: right off the cob, as popcorn, or ground into tortillas or cornmeal. The most widely grown crop in the United States today is **corn**: there are nearly **90 million** acres of corn, which is about the size of Germany! But most of these crops are not the kind of corn you roast on the grill and eat! Most corn goes to feeding **livestock** or is processed into things like sweeteners, cereal, cornstarch, and ethanol, a car fuel.

Agritourism—tourism on the farm—connects people to the land and, at the same time, helps small farms stay financially healthy so they can keep their animals and plants healthy.

There were 600 **tractors** in the United States in 1907. Today there are about 4.7 million.

Scarecrows work best in the spring, to protect newly sown fields: that's when crows like to nibble young shoots or peck for seeds in the soil.

HARVEST SEASON FUN

Hay rides, pick-your-own pumpkin patches, and corn mazes: farms take on new life in October, when farmers are finished harvesting their main crops and can open their farms to visitors. Test your sense of direction by plunging into a **corn maze!** Mazes typically have miles of trails in them and cover several acres of ground. Or pick the perfect **pumpkin** to take home to carve or to bake a pie. Maybe you'll find one as big as the world's largest: in 2016, Mathias Willemijns of Belgium grew a pumpkin that weighed **2,323 pounds** (1,054 kg)!

BiGFOOT

Found on the Farm

1 BigFoot

1 Legendary Footprint

14 Yellow Maze Walkers

4 Busy Farmers

3 Mrs. Farmers

9 Diving Barn Swallows

14 Clucking Hens

5 Happy Scarecrows

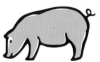

13 Pinky Pigs

Camping

HOW TO CAMP

People go **"camping"** in different ways: in an **RV** (recreational vehicle) that's kind of like a tiny house on wheels; in a **cabin** in a country setting; or in the great outdoors sleeping on the ground or in a hammock. Most people, however, pitch a **tent** in a rented space, usually in a campground that has a bathroom and shower available. Campgrounds often have a pool to enjoy, as well as activities like volleyball, a playground, shuffleboard, and campfire activities (s'mores! singing! storytelling!).

WHAT TO BRING

Top must-haves for every camping trip:

Cooler, to keep perishable foods refrigerated over the weekend

Bug spray, for those mosquito swarms at dusk

Lantern, for nighttime card games

Flip-flops, for the public showers

Sleeping bag, for snugness at night

> The most popular camping region in America is in the Rocky Mountains.

CAMPING WITH MARSHMALLOWS

Marshmallows were practically made for the campfire! These sweet treats originally came from the white, sticky sap of the root of a swamp-loving plant called the **marsh mallow.** Nowadays, marshmallows are made of corn syrup, cane sugar, and gelatin. The best way to roast a marshmallow is to hold it near **hot coals** rather than over flames. The surface will turn brown (but not burned black, hopefully!), and the gelatin and sugar will get a little **gooey**—perfect for adding to graham crackers and chocolate to make **s'mores!**

To build their canoes, Native American tribes used hollowed-out tree trunks.

BOATING BY MUSCLE POWER

Many campers **tow** their own boats to a campsite, or they **rent** one at their destination. Being on the water in a boat that you move yourself (no engine!) is a **peaceful** way to see things you may not have noticed before. Put on your **life jacket** and go for a ride!

Canoe (top photo): A skinny boat between 10 and 20 feet (3–6 m) long, the canoe has two or three seats. Canoe paddles have only one blade, and it takes two people paddling in rhythm to really make a canoe move smoothly.

Kayak (middle photo): Kayaks are made of plastic and are usually built for just one person, though some have two seats. Kayak paddles have two blades instead of one. The paddler sits with legs extended and moves the paddle from the left to right side of the kayak in a kind of figure-8 motion.

Rowboat (bottom photo): Most rowboats have two single-bladed oars attached to the sides of the boat. One person can row by leaning backward and pulling on the oar handles, and passengers can relax and enjoy the ride—until it's their turn to row!

BEAR VISITORS

The **black bear** is an unwanted guest in some campgrounds. Bears are very smart and have excellent sight and smell—they will be able to take any food left out at a campsite, even if you think it's safe in a cooler. Your best bet is to store food in the **trunk** of a car or in a **sealed bag** hung on a rope stretched between 2 trees. If a black bear does show up, campers can usually chase it away by yelling, waving, and banging pans.

Coolers are NOT bear-proof.

STORE ALL FOOD IN VEHICLES

BiGFOOT

Goes Camping

1 BigFoot

1 Legendary Footprint

5 Curious Bird-watchers

7 Bucky Beavers

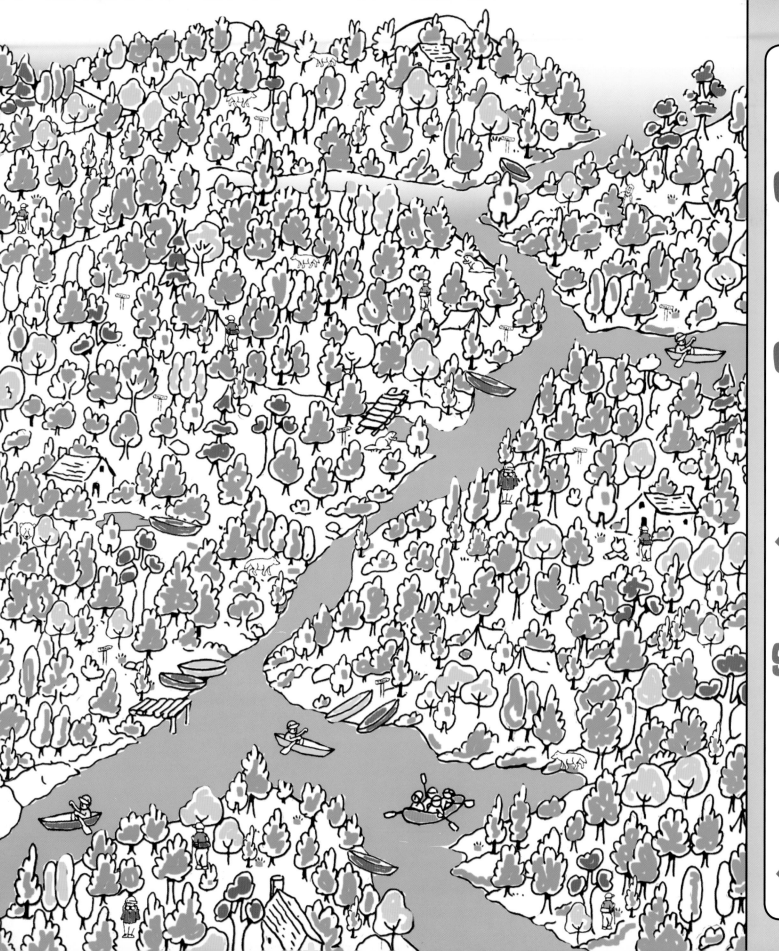

6 Orange-Jacket Hikers

6 Blue-Jacket Hikers

1 Bashful Bear

9 Wandering Coyotes

1 Massive Moose

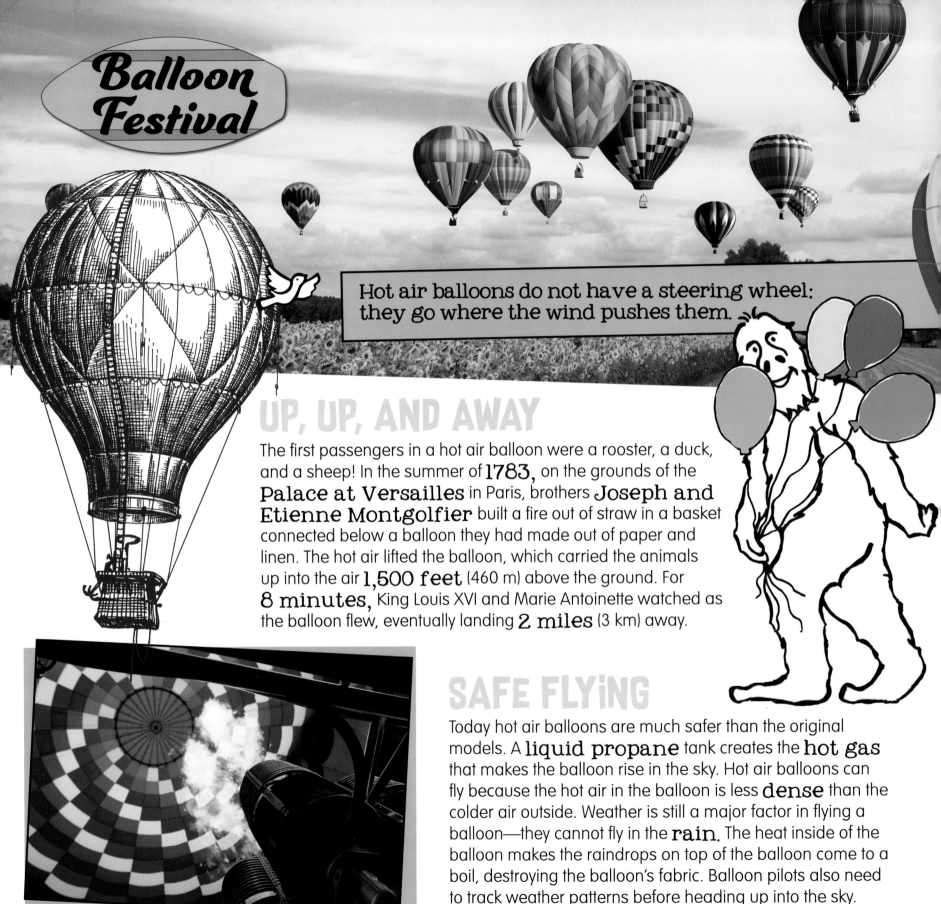

Balloon Festival

Hot air balloons do not have a steering wheel: they go where the wind pushes them.

UP, UP, AND AWAY

The first passengers in a hot air balloon were a rooster, a duck, and a sheep! In the summer of **1783,** on the grounds of the **Palace at Versailles** in Paris, brothers **Joseph and Etienne Montgolfier** built a fire out of straw in a basket connected below a balloon they had made out of paper and linen. The hot air lifted the balloon, which carried the animals up into the air **1,500 feet** (460 m) above the ground. For **8 minutes,** King Louis XVI and Marie Antoinette watched as the balloon flew, eventually landing **2 miles** (3 km) away.

SAFE FLYING

Today hot air balloons are much safer than the original models. A **liquid propane** tank creates the **hot gas** that makes the balloon rise in the sky. Hot air balloons can fly because the hot air in the balloon is less **dense** than the colder air outside. Weather is still a major factor in flying a balloon—they cannot fly in the **rain.** The heat inside of the balloon makes the raindrops on top of the balloon come to a boil, destroying the balloon's fabric. Balloon pilots also need to track weather patterns before heading up into the sky.

In 2016, Fedor Konyukhov (Russia) flew a hot air balloon around the world in 11 days—only the 4th person to ever do that!

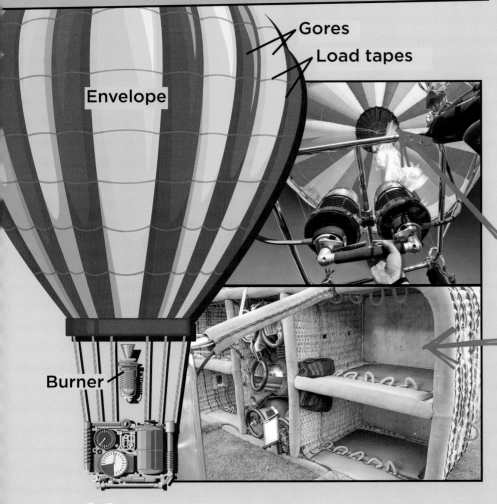

Envelope

Gores

Load tapes

Burner

PARTS OF THE HOT AIR BALLOON

Envelope: The big, colorful balloon part that holds the air. The first envelopes were made of cloth; modern envelopes are made of heat-resistant nylon and coated on the inside with silicon.

Load tapes: Vertical and horizontal strips that help the envelope lift the weight of the basket.

Gores: In the envelope, the panels of fabric between the load tapes.

Parachute valve: A hole in the top of the balloon that is kept sealed during flight. The pilot can use a cord to unseal it and let the air out to make the balloon go down.

Basket: Where passengers and equipment ride. Modern hot air balloons have wicker baskets made of woven willow, an extremely lightweight yet sturdy material. Steel cords reinforce the basket and connect it to the load tapes.

Burner: The propane-fueled stove that shoots hot air up into the envelope.

BALLOON BONANZA

Albuquerque, New Mexico, is home to the largest annual international hot air balloon festival in the world. The **9-day** event has over **700 balloons** each year. But New Mexico isn't the only place where balloon fans gather. There are over 200 hot air balloon festivals across the globe every year. In 2010, **Christian Brown** exhibited and flew a few lucky passengers in his glass-bottomed hot air balloon at the Bristol (England) International Balloon Fiesta. Imagine looking down and seeing only a bit of clear glass between you and the ground far below. Mr. Brown told the media that the flight was **"terrifying"**!

BiGFOOT
Joins a Balloon Festival

1 BigFoot

1 Legendary Footprint

15 Green Balloons

1 Pink-Shirt Lady

1 Yellow Balloon Watcher

2 Girls with Heart Balloons

3 Balloon Sellers

8 Happy Doves

9 Feeding Pigeons

HISTORY OF MINI-GOLF

Many believe the world's **oldest** miniature (mini)-golf course was established in 1867 at **The Ladies' Putting Club** of St. Andrews, in Scotland. While the course didn't have waterfalls and windmills, there were plenty of real **rabbit holes** and a small path was often flooded—a challenging mini-golf course even for today's players!

Mini-golf as we know it now most likely began in **Chattanooga**, Tennessee, in the late 1920s. **Garnet Carter**, owner of the Fairyland Hotel, built a mini-golf course called **"Tom Thumb on Lookout Mountain."** Carter's course had garden gnomes for scenery and hollow logs and rock tunnels as hazards (obstacles). Soon mini-golf fever spread across America! Mini-golf courses sprang up everywhere, even on rooftops in New York City. By 1930, there were **25,000** courses in the country. Today there are about 5,000 mini-golf courses in the United States.

MINI-GOLF CAPITAL OF THE WORLD?

There are about **50** miniature golf courses in **Myrtle Beach**, South Carolina, which is only about 17 square miles (44 km^2). It's so competitive that mini-golf course owners build more and more **complex** obstacles and scenery every year. Examples include Elvis statues, abominable snowmen, downed planes, mermaids, pirate ships sitting in coves, erupting volcanoes, robotic dinosaurs, sea monster skeletons, Aztec ruins, and, of course, the classic windmill. Which one do you want to try?

HOW TO PUTT

Putting is when you gently hit the ball with the club so it goes across the green and into the hole. It is part hand-eye coordination and part concentration. Experts urge putters to **first imagine sinking the shot.** It builds confidence as well as gives some idea of how hard to hit the ball. **Grip is the next important part.** The palm of the dominant hand and the back of the weaker hand both should point toward the hole. Both thumbs should line up on top of the club's handle. Once the grip and stance are set, it's time to **block out all distractions,** take a deep breath, and swing. Following through, or continuing the swing after the ball has been struck, helps ensure the ball goes where it's supposed to go.

September 21 is National Miniature Golf Day in the USA.

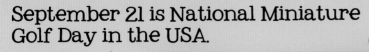

KEEPING SCORE

Before any game of mini-golf can begin, someone must be elected **scorekeeper.** That person is in charge of carrying the **scorecard** and the little **pencil** from the caddy house and recording everyone's scores after each hole. It helps to know some golf terms that real golfers use.

Par: This number is how many strokes it's supposed to take to sink the ball in the hole.

Birdie: One under par. Good job!

Eagle: Two under par. Great job!

Hole-in-one: One stroke, and the ball is in. Amazing job!

Bogey: One over par. Uh oh!

Double and triple bogey: Two and three over par. Not good!

Choke: When it's all going so well and then it isn't; usually due to nerves.

BiGFOOT
at Mini-Golf World

1 BigFoot

1 Legendary Footprint

18 Red Flags

10 Pink Flamingos

6 Yellow-Dress Golfers

2 Passing Doves

6 Focused Putters

3 Green Golf Balls

2 Girls with Heart Balloons

6 Hungry Alligators

ANSWER KEY

Even in the biggest cities of the world, far from his home habitat, BigFoot is an expert at staying lost. He climbs roofs, hides behind buildings, blends into crowds—it's tricky work finding him! If you were stumped the first time around, you can use this guide—the **small red dot** shows where his elusive footprint is, while the **big red dot** in each picture reveals BigFoot himself. Just as in real life, the people, animals, and objects are easier to spot than finding BigFoot, so they are not included in this answer key.

BigFoot

Legendary Footprint

Cruise

Carnival

African Plains

Deep Sea Diving

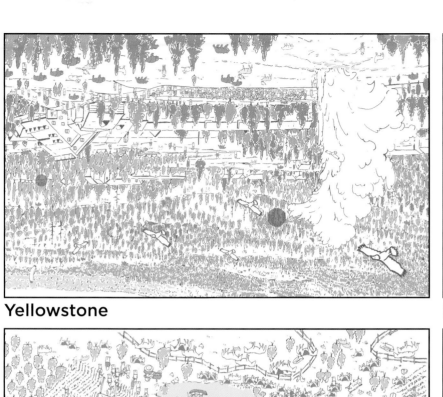

Yellowstone

Beach

Farm

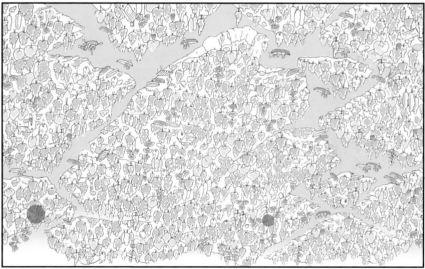

Camping

Balloon Festival

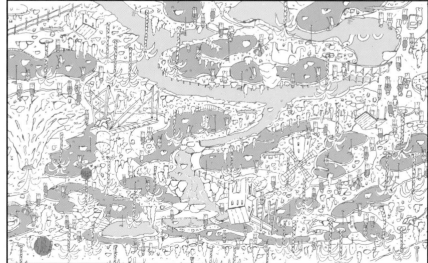

Mini-Golf World

ABOUT THE ARTiST

As with BigFoot, the artist and creator of this series is a bit on the elusive side. He is rarely seen in public, spending most of his days sketching in his studio located among the mighty oak trees found only in the deep, dark woods far off the beaten path.

Deeply inspired by nature, the artist spent most of his childhood tracking creatures great and small across the rocky ridgelines and wooded mountainsides, perfecting his tracking skills and keen ability to spot what many of us never see. It was once said that the artist could identify approaching hummingbirds from two counties away with one eye, while tracking a fast-moving, bouncing black bear on a pogo stick with the other eye.

Despite his many accomplishments, his most important discovery and skill is the ability to spot the deceptive BigFoot that walks among us but remains unseen by most. After spending decades learning the habits of this elusive, mythical creature, the tracker/artist has finally agreed to share his journals that capture the sightings of the infamous, larger-than-life creature that has mystified generations.

Now you have the opportunity to sharpen your search-and-find skills by finding not only BigFoot and his legendary footprint, but also the many other unusual and sometimes unexpected people, creatures, and objects that can be found at anytime . . . anywhere.

Happy Searching!